50 Rules for Sons

By Tim Hoch

II

50 Rules for Sons

By Tim Hoch

U.S. Copyright Registration Number 1-599761491

www.50rulesforsons.com

Published by:
Improvisation Partners, LP
5616 Malvey Avenue
Fort Worth, Texas 76107

First Edition © 2013 by Tim Hoch
Softcover ISBN: 978-0-9849702-0-9
Ebook ISBN: 978-0-9849702-1-6

Because of the dynamic nature of the Internet, any Web addresses or links contained within this work may have changed since original publication and may no longer be valid.

Events portrayed within this work actually took place. However, all of the names, places, and organizations have been changed.

IV

50 Rules for Sons

DEDICATION

It would be impossible to list all of the people who helped shape the lessons in this book, but this is for my parents, my wife and my kids who have taught me more than I could ever put in writing.

RULE 01

Take stock of where you've been but don't dwell on it.

4

RULE 02

Don't let a painful past own you, but keep the scars from the past close at hand. They're part of you.

RULE 03

Set goals and work like hell to accomplish them. Later you'll realize the journey was far more enjoyable than the end result.

RULE 04

Offer those less fortunate a helping hand even though some may not appreciate it.

RULE 05

In business, it's best to try and get along. But remember there are some people you will run across who don't understand anything but a hard kick in the balls. Make sure your aim is good.

RULE 06

Don't ever assume that others are looking out for your best interest. Some people are. Most people are not. If you find someone who is, guard and treasure that relationship above all others.

RULE 07

Be open to, and unashamed of, the possibility that you might be wrong.

RULE 08

Take a back road trip through California. Take a good playlist (heavy on Jerry Jeff Walker), a journal and a camera (on second thought, never mind the camera).

RULE 09

Volunteer because you want to, not because you feel like you have to.

RULE 10

Develop your spiritual side but do not be a slave to form or ritual. Cultivate your own relationship with God.

RULE 11

Understand the importance of leverage. Don't borrow more than you can afford to pay back.

RULE 12

Doing good is equally
as important as
doing well.

RULE 13

Time is your only commodity. Don't waste it. And don't give it to people or projects that don't respect it.

RULE 14

Try new things – daily.

RULE 15

Be decisive.

RULE 16

Do what you love but find a way to make money doing it or you won't be able to do it very long.

34

RULE 17

Don't be an ideologue
or a demagogue.
The world has
plenty of those.

36

RULE 18

Don't vote straight ticket. Think for yourself. If you think one political party has all of the answers, you're not asking the right questions.

RULE 19

Don't buy into dogmatic bullshit. Opinions are not facts.

RULE 20

Give people the benefit of the doubt, until you doubt the benefit.

RULE 21

Most of your life
should be spent
running uphill. If not,
you're not challenging
yourself.

RULE 22

Don't bring home stray kittens. Someone other than you is probably better equipped to take care of them.

RULE 23

Most of your life your
only company is
yourself. Like yourself.

RULE 24

If you want to get
a tattoo, go to your
closet and pick out
your favorite shirt.
Wear it every day and
every night for 2 years.
If you're not tired of
wearing it after 2 years,
go get your tattoo.

RULE 25

Don't worry about trying to impress people with your knowledge or experience when you're young. Just be interested, engaged and eager to learn.

RULE 26

If you show up to class on time and sit in one of the first three rows, you will succeed.

RULE 27

It's often easier to effectuate change by working within the system rather than outside the system. When it's not, be sure to find strong allies.

RULE 28

If the police officer or the professor is talking, you're listening.

RULE 29

It isn't always chess; sometimes it's just checkers.

RULE 30

In things both big and small, always be someone upon whom others can rely. Help your friend move into his new apartment. Return phone calls. Keep your word. Follow through.

RULE 31

Read leisurely for at least 30 minutes every day. This will broaden your point of view and increase your curiosity about the world.

RULE 32

Kindness can be disarming.

RULE 33

Stand up straight, look people square in the eye and be the first to offer a firm handshake.

RULE 34

Keep a toothbrush
and toothpaste close
at hand. A vigorous
brushing before an
important meeting is a
confidence builder.

RULE 35

Don't talk about how much ass you kicked in high school. No one gives a damn.

RULE 36

You're always working
for yourself, even
when you're working
for someone else.

RULE 37

Don't assume that an obvious question has already been asked.

RULE 38

When reviewing
a proposal from
someone else, don't
feel constrained by
its parameters.

RULE 39

Embrace and celebrate
the things that make
you feel different from
everyone else.

RULE 40

Resist the insidious,
slow progression
toward cynicism.

RULE 41

Don't get frustrated just because your immediate needs are not the priority of others. They seldom will be.

RULE 42

If you see someone who is alone, go out of your way to tell them hello.

RULE 43

Buy a box of nice
stationery and
write "thank you"
and "thinking of you"
notes often.

RULE 44

Look for beauty in the mundane.

RULE 45

Always carry cash.

RULE 46

Wait at least 24 hours before sending a letter with the salutation "Dear Judge Dumb Ass."

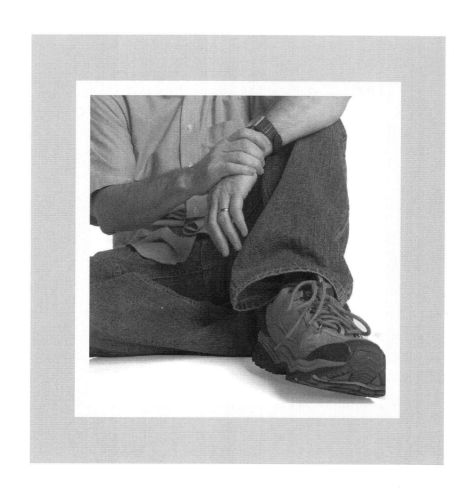

RULE 47

Pay your fair share.
Don't be a moocher.

RULE 48

Don't major in the minors.

RULE 49

Exercise regularly.

RULE 50

No matter what
is in front of you,
walk toward it with
confidence.

BACK STORIES

Each rule within
this book has a
story behind it, an
experience that left
a lasting impression
on me. I thought that
this book would not
be complete without
providing you with
a brief explanation of
each rule.

RULE 01: *Take stock of where you've been but don't dwell on it.*

BACKSTORY: This is about looking forward. As I accumulate life experiences I am tempted to put these experiences on mental replay. This is a dangerous waste of time and energy, especially when the loop is negative. I have made thousands of mistakes and I have tons of regret. But I try to accept it, learn from it and move on. In the words of the great Cherokee proverb: Don't let yesterday use up too much of today.

RULE 02: *Don't let a painful past own you, but keep the scars from the past*

BACKSTORY: I know a man whose son committed suicide. I ran into him a few years after his son's death and asked how he was doing.

"Of course it has been difficult but in a lot of ways I have grown. I've had so many people share their own experiences with suicide. I never had any idea that so many people were carrying around so much pain. My perspective is much different. I have an awareness and an appreciation now that I didn't have before."

Because of his pain, he developed a deeper understanding of himself. He had a greater appreciation for life, his family and for things that matter. Pain can make us more compassionate, understanding people. It can give us a depth of character we would not otherwise have. The only way to turn tragedy into a positive is to learn from it, grow because of it and help ease the pain of others with it.

RULE 03: *Set goals and work like hell to accomplish them. But later you'll realize the journey was a lot more enjoyable than the end result.*

BACKSTORY: Think of every major goal you have ever achieved, every success you have ever enjoyed. Chances are you will look most fondly on the things that seemed so inconsequential at the time. Funny comments, crazy twists, serendipitous moments. When my son was a junior in high school his football team won the conference championship. One evening I was visiting with several of the players and I asked them to recall their favorite memory from the season. Locker room pranks, pep rallies, even two-a-day practices were mentioned. Interestingly, very few spoke about the actual Championship game.

This is a beautiful paradox of life. We spend so much time preparing for our big events. But ninety nine percent of our enjoyment comes from the in-betweens. Relish those in betweens. As Warren Zevon neared death from cancer he was asked whether he had any advice for others. His simple response: "Enjoy every sandwich."

RULE 04: *Offer those less fortunate a helping hand even though some may not appreciate it.*

BACKSTORY: I once took my family to help serve Thanksgiving dinner at a local homeless shelter. We stood there for a few hours in the serving line, then we cleaned the dining area. What a magnanimous, selfless gesture on our part. After we finished I expected that we would be detained for several hours basking in the adoration of huddled masses. Instead we were met with an almost palpable indifference. This was an embarrassing lesson in humility. Or a humiliating lesson in embarrassment. Choose one. Either way my egotistical approach to those less fortunate is still difficult to retell. Here's what I've since come to understand. Helping others should be a truly selfless act. If you are doing it for any other reason, do NOT do it. Those who are less fortunate are not there to assuage your guilt or make you feel better about yourself. And they do not "owe" you anything in return for your generosity. Not a handshake, not a smile, not a thank you... nothing.

RULE 05: *In business, it's best to try and get along. But remember there are some people you will run across who don't understand anything but a hard kick in the balls. Make sure your aim is good.*

BACKSTORY: The world has an inordinate number of manipulative, self-centered, even malevolent jerks. You will, no doubt, encounter your fair share of them. Plain and simple, these people must be dealt with forcefully. Here are a few tips for dealing with these people:

1. Usually, there is an emotional component that underlies a difficult temperament. Try to remove or neutralize the emotion.

2. Do not make a threat unless you are willing and able to follow through.

3. Consider putting every communication in writing.

Not everyone will have the same understanding of the rules of decorum and fair play. But, successful people learn how to deal with difficult people and are not afraid to do so.

RULE 06: *Don't ever assume that others are looking out for your best interest. Some people are. Most people are not. If you find someone who is, guard and treasure that relationship above all others.*

BACKSTORY: Each of us has been at the absolute center of every experience we have ever had. Our world has unfolded directly in front of us. So it is natural to assume that the world revolves around us. It doesn't. And this can be a hard lesson to learn.

When I graduated from law school I was looking for a job. The hiring partner for a law firm took me to lunch. While we were at lunch we ran into the father of a friend who I had known for quite some time. The hiring partner knew this man as well. The rest of the lunch I felt secure with the knowledge that our mutual relationship would lead to a lucrative offer. The interview really could not have gone any better.

A few days later the hiring partner called and said that he would not be able to make an offer. I was devastated. I wondered what happened so I called my friend's father to see if he would try to salvage my opportunity. He never called me back. Later I learned that he had, in fact, spoken with the hiring partner and torpedoed my chance. To this very day, I never learned why.

Bottom line: Don't wait for your opportunity. Seize it for yourself. Be self sufficient. If you are relying solely on the kindness of others to get ahead you'll be waiting a long, long time.

RULE 07: *Be open to, and unashamed of, the possibility that you might be wrong.*

BACKSTORY: This rule is deeper than it appears. This is not about realizing past mistakes. This is about being aware of present tense wrongness. The skill set that you used to arrive at a decision is the same skill set you are using to evaluate whether you are correct in that decision. We tend to shape reality to comport with our own perceptions. And our perceptions are very often mistaken.

As a lawyer I have had the privilege of working in a number of different areas. Real estate, pharmaceuticals, taxes, insurance, trucking, patents, investments etc. I am astonished by the number of topics about which I not only had no prior knowledge but hardly even knew existed.

In other words, there are things we know. There are things we don't know. And there are things we don't even know we don't know. I am reminded of this more than I care to admit.

RULE 08: *Take a backroad trips through California. Take a good playlist (heavy on Jerry Jeff Walker), a journal and a camera (on second thought, never mind the camera).*

BACKSTORY: It often seems as though the world is at our fingertips. We can connect with anyone, anywhere in the world within a few seconds. We can get to the airport and end up on the other side of the country in a few hours. This leads to the mistaken notion that we live in a entirely knowable, compact universe.

Nothing reminds me of the expansive greatness of this world like a road trip. Being at ground level and meeting others where they are can be a wonderful, even enlightening, experience. I believe it is imperative to get outside of our world. Explore the open road. Go without a plan. Or a GPS. Or a camera. A camera forces us to plan and pose our moments. In order to truly get away, we need to immerse ourselves in the adventure.

RULE 09: *Volunteer because you want to, not because you feel like you have to.*

BACKSTORY: I was once asked to serve on a building committee at my church. I know very little about construction, but I wanted to get to know some of the other members, so I joined. We met 8 times over a 2 year period and I believe it is fair to say that my contribution was negligible. I was on the committee for the wrong reasons and it was reflected in my lack of meaningful input. My original reason for joining the committee (i.e. to meet and impress a few influential people) was an unqualified failure, as well.

Unless you can make something better, do not volunteer for it.

RULE 10: *Develop your spiritual side but do not be a slave to form or ritual. Cultivate your own relationship with God.*

BACKSTORY: I've always found it interesting that the most intimate part of our life-our very soul- is often made to conform to a preordained set of beliefs. This is not a knock on religion. Indeed religion can give a nice framework upon which we can build our faith. Unfortunately religion can also be used as a way to manipulate people.

It is imperative that we find our own way regarding our spirituality. Go beyond the customs of our church. Ask difficult questions about our beliefs. Above all, respect the beliefs of others.

RULE 11: *Understand the importance of leverage. Don't borrow more than you can afford to pay back.*

BACKSTORY: The single most important reason for the growth of America has been the plentiful and relatively cheap access to capital i.e. the ability to borrow money. Taking on debt is not a problem. Taking on debt you have no means to repay is a problem.

Even if I am borrowing money that requires no personal guaranty, I treat it as though it does. Of course, there are many situations where a failure to repay debt has nothing to do with a failure of accountability. But handling borrowed money with utmost care can greatly minimize these occasions.

RULE 12: *Doing good is equally as important as doing well.*

BACKSTORY: When I was a kid, both of my parents worked. They hired a beautiful black woman named Eather to care for my brothers, sister and me. She was in her late sixties when I was going through my pre teenage years. She was a perfect combination of sweet and strict.

After I had been a lawyer for several years my Mom called to tell me that Eather was ill. Eather was in her late nineties when I dropped in to visit during a trip home.

Eather gave me a big hug. "So glad to see you Timmy, how are you doing?" she asked.

"I'm doing good Eather."

"Oh I'm so glad to hear that." She paused and looked into my eyes. "I hope you always do good."

With brevity and charm Eather was able to impart two quick lessons; the first was a lesson in grammar, the second was a lesson in life. It doesn't matter how well you are doing if you are not doing any good. I'll never possess the innate goodness of Eather Peachlin, but her lessons will always be dear to me.

RULE 13: *Time is your only commodity. Don't waste it. And, don't give it to people or projects that don't respect it.*

BACKSTORY: We will be able to bargain for just about everything we want during our lifetime, except time.

These past few years I have started to keep track of, and evaluate, how I spend my time. I try to avoid people who waste my time. It has made me more appreciative of, and responsive to, the people who value my time. It has also made me a more productive person.

This rule applies to everything. The most important decision we will make each day is how we choose to spend our time. Spend wisely because it's never coming back.

RULE 14: *Try new things – daily.*

BACKSTORY: Be open-minded.

111

RULE 15: *Be decisive.*

BACKSTORY: The universal hallmark of a good leader is decisiveness. This is an under appreciated trait. People want someone who will stand up and make a decision no matter the consequences. I have witnessed some critical thinkers who are very astute decision makers. Here are a few things I have learned from them.

1. Rely on your core values. This will serve as the foundation for your decision and will typically make your decision easier.

2. Rely on hard facts but do not over analyze. Input from a few trusted resources is usually enough.

3. Once you have made your decision, own your decision.

The world is looking for leaders who are willing to support, defend and be held accountable for their decisions.

RULE 16: *Do what you love but find a way to make money doing it or you won't be able to do it very long.*

BACKSTORY: People often say "Do what you love, the money will follow." I would like to add a very important caveat. Not necessarily.

I once loved acting. I was in every high school play. I was good, but I wasn't great. I wasn't devoted to the craft in a way that would ensure either success or happiness. Put another way, many baseball players long to play in the major leagues but the odds of making it are about one in 500,000. A better approach is to identify your talents and develop them in a way that allows you to choose a career where you will excel. When you are unable to be a movie star or a professional athlete, it will be more important to love what you do than to do what you love.

RULE 17: *Don't be an ideologue or a demagogue. The world has plenty of those.*

BACKSTORY: We are all in a position at some point in our lives to wield influence over others. This is a position of enormous responsibility- one that will require complete authenticity and transparency.

This requires us to eschew agendas and manipulation. This is difficult to do. And I have failed a number of times to live up to this standard. It takes harsh self analysis and honesty.

RULE 18: *Don't vote straight ticket. Think for yourself. If you think one political party has all of the answers, you're not asking the right questions.*

BACKSTORY: There are thousands of divergent views on a multitude of issues but only two political parties to advance those views. The extremists in both parties have completely hijacked any honest debate on these issues.

Politics have always been the theater of the absurd. When we decide who to support by watching the same television shows or reading the same newspapers, we are living in an echo chamber.

Voting straight ticket is lazy and irresponsible. Our right to vote requires more from us than blind devotion. Do your homework; ask tough questions not only about what a candidate believes but about what we believe. Vote for someone, not against someone.

RULE 19: *Don't buy into dogmatic bullshit. Opinions are not facts.*

BACKSTORY: Facts are empirically verifiable truths. Opinions are beliefs that may or may not be true. Beware of opinions masquerading as fact. I am astounded at the number of people who fail to recognize the difference.

RULE 20: *Give people the benefit of the doubt, until you doubt the benefit.*

BACKSTORY: A friend of mine runs an investment fund. When he started his fund he asked me to invest in one of his deals. He is a smart, capable guy so I did. Within a year I had an uneasy feeling. There was very little communication, so I asked him to lunch. During lunch he gave a glowing report about the investment and, in fact, had a second deal he wanted me to see. Overlooking common sense and the faint but unmistakable chime of warning bells, I went back for more.

Shortly thereafter I approached him about an idea that I had which fit his investment profile. He liked the idea so much he invested in a carbon copy of my idea-with someone else. No more benefit of the doubt.

I lost my entire investment in the two original deals. But I won't lose any money on any future deals with him and I learned a valuable lesson along the way. I consider it a net positive.

114

RULE 21: *Most of your life should be spent running uphill. If not, you're not challenging yourself.*

BACKSTORY: There is a term used in business called "reversion to the mean." I'm not certain of the correct business definition but my own working definition is "the tendency, over time, to find a comfortable station and fail to deviate too far from there." We find a job and settle in. We gravitate toward a comfortable routine. Sure we do things once in awhile that take us outside of our zone but we do not really elevate the plane.

The battle against complacency is constant and requires vigilance. That is why it is important to constantly find new challenges.

RULE 22: *Don't bring home stray kittens. Someone other than you is probably better equipped to take care of them.*

BACKSTORY: Stray cats choose to live in the wild. They refuse domestication. They are opportunistic and predatory. They should only be handled by trained professionals.

Because I have tried to take in a few stray cats over the years, I have learned this the hard way.

I represented a client who was about to have his house foreclosed, a single dad with two teenagers. Unemployed. Terrible credit. He needed a restraining order to prevent the foreclosure so we set up an appointment on an emergency basis. He was extremely late for his first appointment with me, which is usually a harbinger of bad things. When he arrived he convinced me of his good intentions, his hard luck and his extreme need. So I took him in.

We successfully postponed the foreclosure. As we tried to work something out with the lender the real story began to emerge. He had made only 2 house payments in the previous 12 months, his employer fired him for excessive absenteeism, his kids lived with his ex-wife and he had a serious dependency problem. In short, he was a mess. Unfortunately, he was my mess. And I was woefully unqualified to help him. He didn't need a lawyer. He needed a therapist.

He was one in a long line of stray cats I have tried to help. And I know this about strays; they will cry for attention, fight like hell if they are cornered and they will gladly accept your generosity. But, stray cats live outside because they choose to. They don't want to have rules. So unless you are trained to rescue stray cats, leave them alone.

RULE 23: *Most of your life your only company is yourself. Like yourself.*

BACKSTORY: There is a huge benefit to spending time alone. We are able to reflect on, and become, the person we wish to be. When we are surrounded by others all the time we simply become a composite of everything they are-the good and the bad. And we never get any rest.

When we spend time alone we have an opportunity to sort through the day's events. We can manage the emotional component of our lives. We can try to make sense of how things fit together and what we need to prioritize.

Unless we engage in self analysis, we will never grow. And self analysis can only be done in quiet solitude.

116

RULE 24: *If you want to get a tattoo, go to your closet and pick out your favorite shirt. Wear it every day and every night for 2 years. If you're not tired of wearing it after 2 years, go get your tattoo.*

BACKSTORY: When I was 8 years old I spent every waking hour playing with match box cars. My favorite match box car wasn't actually a car, it was a motorcycle- a chopper to be exact-complete with yellow and orange flames painted on the gas tank. I carried that chopper with me everywhere I went. One day I got some markers and drew a fake tattoo replica of the flames on my bicep. My mom commented, "you're lucky that isn't permanent ink." She's never been so right.

A few years later I had my first love. She bought me a pooka shell necklace. I wore it every day for about ninety consecutive days. From day 2 through day 89 I would have agreed to permanently imbed a pooka shell in each of my nostrils just to prove my devotion. On the 90th day, I would not have been quite so willing.

I don't have enough dermis to hold the various tattoo images I might have taken over the years. The rock band KISS, the movie Footloose, the television show Miami Vice, the Jackson 5.

They range from the embarrassing to the ridiculous and they all share a single unifying trait. They were transitory. Your life is a series of stages, each one of which, if you're lucky, you'll outgrow.

RULE 25: *Don't worry about trying to impress people with your knowledge or experience when you're young. Just be interested, engaged and eager to learn.*

BACKSTORY: As a business owner, I have interviewed a number of people over the years. Usually I ask a few questions about experience. Then I ask them whether they have any questions about my company or our industry. I am astounded at the number of people who say: "No."

This is the most telling part of the interview. Your questions will usually tell me more about your potential than your resume. Your questions should be specific and pointed. Here are some examples:

1. I read "x" about your company, can you tell me more about that?

2. What do you believe is the biggest opportunity for your company's growth over the next year and how can this position contribute to that growth?

3. What are the biggest challenges your company faces? Is there a way I can contribute to meeting those challenges?

I would rather hire someone who is eager to learn than someone who already knows everything.

RULE 26: If you show up to class on time and sit in one of the first three rows, you will succeed.

BACKSTORY: Participate. Ask questions. Learn the subject. Understand where the topic fits into the big picture. A friend of mine is a head hunter. He places people in upper management positions. One of his favorite questions for prospects is: "Why didn't you get a 4.0 in college?"

He does not mean to suggest that every one of his candidates must have straight A's. Not at all. But if they don't, he wants a damn good explanation about why not. If we take responsibility for all of the variables we can control, we will have a satisfactory answer for that question.

RULE 27: *It's often easier to effectuate change by working within the system rather than outside the system. When it's not, be sure to find strong allies.*

BACKSTORY: I once served on the Board of a charity when a local group of citizens began to question our very successful parenting program. They were concerned that federal tax dollars were being used to fund abortions. They organized a protest and contacted the local news media. A three day frenzy ensued. But there was a big problem. They were wrong. No monies were being used to fund abortions but it sure sounded like a good story. A few years later the leader of this group of citizens tried to join the Board. She had no credibility within the organization and was turned down.

Obviously, she would have been much more effective if she had done her research. But assume for a minute that our organization was, in fact, using federal funds for abortions. Was her approach the most effective way to urge a policy change? I don't think so.

If you see something wrong with your kid's school, stop complaining about it to the other parents. Go to the administration. Still not satisfied? Run for School Board. If you don't like the way your city is spending money, run for city council. Working from the inside is typically the most effective way to get results.

RULE 28: *If the police officer or the professor is talking, you're listening.*

BACKSTORY: There is a good story here which involves a police officer and a guy with a big mouth, but I can't tell it while my kids are still young.

RULE 29: *It isn't always chess; sometimes it's just checkers.*

BACKSTORY: I like to strategize. I analyze situations and try to anticipate roadblocks and problems in an effort to gain a competitive advantage. This may sound strange but this is not always the most effective approach.

I once represented a businessman who wanted to purchase a competitor. We began to map out ways to accomplish this. Should we buy enough shares to threaten a change in management or even a takeover? Should we hire his key employees? Should we target his biggest client?

After a few meetings my client simply said, "Why don't I just call and ask him whether he wants to sell?"

Hell of an idea. That phone call led to an eventual merger which led to the formation of an extremely successful business. Checkers, not chess.

RULE 30: *In things both big and small, always be someone upon whom others can rely. Help your friend move into his new apartment. Return phone calls. Keep your word. Follow through.*

BACKSTORY: Here is a question we should ask our good friends: "If you needed help, who would you call?" Our name should be among the first 3 names mentioned. If it is not, then we need to either convey a deeper sense of reliability to that friend or evaluate our relationship with that person.

The people I can trust with the little things will soon be the people I call for the big things.

RULE 31: *Read leisurely for at least 30 minutes every day. This will broaden your point of view and increase your curiosity about the world.*

BACKSTORY: What is the single most important key to success? Curiosity. Unfortunately, we can't teach curiosity. But we can encourage it and cultivate it. Reading is the single best way to do this.

I never used to read anything but the local newspaper or an occasional Sports Illustrated article. Then in the mid 1990s my legal assistant gave me a copy of Angela's Ashes. I started to read it and it was almost like hearing music for the first time. It literally opened my eyes to a different world. The only intellectual exercise that can do that for you is reading.

Over the years I have developed a deep appreciation for reading and my curiosity about the world has grown exponentially. Reading gives us an awareness and a perspective that we would not otherwise enjoy.

RULE 32: *Kindness can be disarming.*

BACKSTORY: I was taking the deposition of an older gentleman in one of my cases and it was not going well. Much to my opponent's delight the witness was extremely combative and difficult and I was doing a poor job of hiding my frustration. During a break I ran into this witness in the rest room. I had learned through my earlier questions that he was from my same hometown, Oklahoma City, so I tentatively started the "do you know" game. Within a few minutes he and I realized we knew many of the same people and by the time we returned to the deposition there was a noticeable change in our relationship. He turned out to be a courteous, pleasant, and helpful witness. Simple kindness will open many doors, even unexpected ones.

RULE 33: *Stand up straight, look people square in the eye and be the first to offer a firm handshake.*

BACKSTORY: I used to find social situations awkward. When introduced to others I was cautious and timid. I admired people who would stand up when approached and reach out their hand with confidence. When I entered the business world I started to understand the importance of this interaction. As goofy as this sounds, I even started to practice my handshake.

Here are some tips about your handshake. First, have dry hands. Second, have a firm, straight on grip. A palm facing upward is a sign of submission; a palm facing downward is a sign of dominance. Third, do not employ the double hand-shake unless you are on intimate terms with the other person. Fourth, maintain eye contact until the handshake is released.

The initial handshake sets the tone for your meeting which sets the tone for your relationship. Do not overlook its importance.

RULE 34: *Keep a toothbrush and toothpaste close at hand. A vigorous brushing before an important meeting is a confidence builder.*

BACKSTORY: The benefits of good hygiene are often under-appreciated until it is too late. Take a shower, wear deodorant, brush your teeth, zip up your pants, trim your nose hairs, shave your neck, clean your ears and shine your shoes. I really do brush my teeth right before every important meeting. I don't want the overriding impression I leave to be bad breath.

RULE 35: *Don't talk about how much ass you kicked in high school. No one gives a damn.*

BACKSTORY: Our greatest accomplishments are our very own. We get to think about them whenever we like. This is a wonderful gift.

But, except for our closest friends, it is not necessarily a gift that other people want to share with us. This is not to say that we should not retell our proudest moments, but one time is enough. Anything more is unbecoming.

RULE 36: *You're always working for yourself, even when you're working for someone else.*

BACKSTORY: There is a man who cleans the floor at the gym where I exercise. It has to be the cleanest floor in the entire State of Texas. He scrutinizes and shines every square inch. For him, the job itself is the reward.

He reminds me of the story of the three brick masons who were working one day when they were approached by a man who asked what they were doing. The first replied, "just laying these bricks." The second man declared, "making a wall." The third exclaimed, "building this beautiful cathedral."

This story illustrates the importance of understanding how your work contributes to the larger picture. Whether you are washing cars or sacking groceries, put your best effort into everything you do. People who matter will notice.

RULE 37: *Don't assume that an obvious question has already been asked.*

BACKSTORY: Early in my legal career I was involved in a lawsuit against a telemarketing firm. This firm used abusive, strong arm sales tactics to dupe consumers into buying insurance policies they did not need. I was working for a seasoned lawyer at the time and he allowed me take the depositions of some of the actual telemarketers. The firm produced a number of files for us to review prior to the depositions. The files appeared clean and made no reference to any of the derogatory tactics which we believed the firm employed. I did notice that a number of acronyms were being used.

I assumed that these acronyms were industry specific terms and since I was reluctant to show ignorance I was hesitant to ask about them. But curiosity got the best of me.

"What does BOHICA stand for?" I asked one telemarketer.

"Wh-where does it say that?" he stammered.

"Down here under the heading 'action required'"
I continued.

He danced around his answer a bit longer before admitting that the acronym stood for "Bend Over, Here it Comes Again."

The seemingly simple question, one which I assumed had an obvious and innocuous answer, put the company on its heels. Other acronyms we learned that day included BMW (Bitch, Moan, Whine); IOWA (Idiot Out Walking About); TLR (Two Legged Rat) and CTD (Circling the Drain). Don't be afraid to ask your question. The answer may prove quite useful.

RULE 38: *When reviewing a proposal from someone else, don't feel constrained its parameters.*

BACKSTORY: When I was trying to settle my first case, as a young lawyer, I received a settlement offer with several items for consideration. I consulted with my client and carefully responded to each separate point before I took my draft to the managing partner. He took a long look at the letter and tore it up. In doing so, he taught me a very important lesson.

When negotiating, the first person to propose the way a deal is structured usually has the upper hand. That person drafts the salient deal points and decides what is left open for discussion. The responding party is simply left to negotiate the blanks. But if you draft the opening offer, you will establish the framework under which a deal will be negotiated.

RULE 39: *Embrace and celebrate the things that make you feel different from everyone else.*

BACKSTORY: I have had this strange obsession with the number eight since I was a kid (probably eight years old). I want to arrange things in groups of eight. The pillow cushions, the lights in the ceiling, the letters on a page. It is a manifestation of obsessive compulsive personality disorder. At one point, it drove me crazy, now I rather enjoy it. Maybe I relish it just to prevent it from driving me crazy.

We all have strange quirks, bizarre behaviors and intrusive thoughts. We often hide or avoid them which takes far more energy than simply acknowledging, dealing and even having fun with them.

RULE 40: *Resist the insidious, slow progression toward cynicism.*

BACKSTORY: Cynicism is inevitable. Delay it as long as possible. Its adverse effects far outweigh the benefits.

RULE 41: *Don't get frustrated just because your immediate needs are not the priority of others. They seldom will be.*

BACKSTORY: Every day we run across people who have the potential to drive us insane. On most occasions we are able to ignore them. That is, unless they stand between us and something we need. The store clerk, the slow driver in the left lane, the airport security screener, the customer service representative, the lady at the DMV… the list is never-ending.

Some simple advice - Do not let these people frustrate you. It is a waste of time and energy. Your exasperation will not cause them to work faster or harder to address your needs. In fact, it will usually have an opposite effect. Occupy your mind with grander ideas than ways in which the DMV can be more efficient.

RULE 42: *If you see someone who is alone, go out of your way to tell them hello.*

BACKSTORY: On the first day of school each year I tell my kids to find someone who is new or who looks like they are having a hard day and say something nice to them. I do this for two reasons. First, it forces my kids to look outward and not inward, particularly on a day that they themselves may be feeling insecure. Second, it creates an expectation of compassion and social interaction.

RULE 43: *Buy a box of nice stationery and write "thank you" and "thinking of you" notes often.*

BACKSTORY: A friend I know was a high school senior when he applied for a college scholarship from a well-known, successful company. His father died a few years earlier and he had to piece together as much financial aid as he could. He landed the scholarship so he sat down and wrote the owner of the company a "thank you" note.

A few days later the owner called my friend. He told him that in all of the years his company had been awarding scholarships, he was the first person to ever send a note. The owner then offered him a summer job. My friend is now 43 years old and has worked for this company ever since. He is now the CEO.

Hand written notes are a lost art. But they make a lasting impression.

RULE 44: *Look for beauty in the mundane.*

BACKSTORY: This is an art that is often reserved for women. My mom, my mother-in-law and my Aunt June had this gift. They could appreciate the deep colors on a leaf, or the descriptive beauty of a well constructed paragraph or the way the sun would reflect through the trees. Sometimes they would see things and comment on them and I would stop in my tracks. This happened when my kids were young as well. How could I miss the smell of the honeysuckle or walk right past the new blooms on a magnolia tree? Or completely ignore the sleeping dog on the porch or the simple sound of the chirping robin?

We are surrounded by divinity. We just have to recognize it.

RULE 45: *Always carry cash.*

BACKSTORY: Several years ago I was driving through a blinding rainstorm in rural Missouri about 100 miles outside of St. Louis when I noticed that I had missed my exit. I drove on for several miles without spotting a place to turn around. That's when I decided to turn around in the grassy median.

Bad move. My tires were completely buried in mud and I was stuck. In the middle of nowhere. Before cell phones. In a downpour.

As luck would have it, a tow truck happened by about 15 minutes later. He pulled up on the shoulder, rolled down his window and asked if he could help. "Yes, yes please," I replied. "Could you just tow me out of the ditch? Once I get on the road I'll be fine."

"No problem. That'll be $50. Cash."

I only had about $10 in wadded up bills. So I appealed to his sense of kindness and hospitality. He had neither.

He said he would try to send along another driver who would take plastic. I knew I would be waiting quite awhile. Finally when the rain subsided I walked several miles to the nearest gas station. I used their ATM and hired a tow truck driver to pull me just a few feet back to the road.

You cannot anticipate all of the times you might be in need of cash. Carry enough to get you to a place where you have credit.

RULE 46: *Wait at least 24 hours before sending a letter with the salutation "Dear Judge Dumb Ass."*

BACKSTORY: When I was a young lawyer I had a particularly contentious case in front of an overbearing Judge. One morning I appeared at a hearing in front of this Judge. He was rude and, in my opinion, flat wrong with respect to his ruling. I thought he needed to know it. I went back to my office and dictated a letter that began: Dear Judge Dumb Ass. I gave the letter to my legal assistant to send.

I slept rather fitfully that night and when I arrived at the office the next day I remarked to my legal assistant that I was starting to regret sending the letter. She reached into her desk drawer and pulled out the letter.

She had the sense to save me from my basest instincts. I have appeared in front of this Judge dozens of times since that day. Some days he is smart, other days he is still pretty dense. Either way, he'll never know what I really think.

RULE 47: *Pay your fair share. Don't be a moocher.*

BACKSTORY: The guy who never has money quickly loses friends. We all know the type- the one who will "get you later," "make it up to you" or "is a little short right now." He is to be avoided. Make sure this person is not you.

RULE 48: *Don't major in the minors.*

BACKSTORY: Being popular. Going to parties. Staying up drinking. Watching television. Constantly checking your cell phone. Gossiping about others. Living for the weekend. This is minor league bullshit for minor league players. Engaging in petty pastimes leads to petty accomplishments.

By all means, it is important to have fun. The point is to put it in proper perspective. If trivial pursuits dominate our time and attention, our accomplishments will be correspondingly minimal.

RULE 49: *Exercise regularly.*

BACKSTORY: Day to day living requires hundreds of incremental choices that will greatly impact our quality of life over the long term. These are simple, almost subconscious choices that turn to habits. The cumulative effect of this may not be readily apparent but the cumulative effect of not doing this can be catastrophic. One of the most important of these is exercise.

The benefits of exercise cannot be overstated. It boosts brain cell survival and delays the onset of neurodegenerative disorders. Studies have shown that exercise is just as effective as medication in treating depression.

I have a replenishment theory about exercise. I believe we are primed to make our best decisions and our strongest impressions when we have a greater sense of well being. When we are tired or out of shape we have a depleted ego. Exercise is the secret ingredient for success.

RULE 50: *No matter what is in front of you, walk toward it with confidence.*

BACKSTORY: There is something magnetic about confidence. In fact, studies confirm that confident people appear more competent. Oftentimes, it is not who you are that allows you to achieve greatness or invite failure, it is who you think you are. Everyone has insecurities, fears and anxieties. What will separate you from others will be your ability to overcome those fears. If you approach every task with confidence you will have a huge advantage over every other person or obstacle you encounter.

Made in the USA
San Bernardino, CA
31 December 2014